Gosport, Indiana 47433

THE SECRET IN THE PEW

Pornography in the Lives of Christian Men

Breaking the Bondage of Sexual Sin

THE SECRET
IN THE PEW

Pornography in the Lives of Christian Men

Breaking the Bondage of Sexual Sin

DAVID A. BLYTHE

Foreword by Tommy Barnett

A Division of WINEPRESS PUBLISHING

Packaged by Pleasant Word, a division of WinePress Publishing, PO Box 428, Enumclaw, WA 98022. The views expressed or implied in this work do not necessarily reflect those of Pleasant Word, a division of WinePress Publishing. The author(s) is ultimately responsible for the design, content and editorial accuracy of this work.

Unless otherwise noted, all Scriptures are taken from the Holy Bible, New International Version, Copyright © 1973, 1978, 1984 by the International Bible Society. Used by permission of Zondervan Publishing House. The "NIV" and "New International Version" trademarks are registered in the United States Patent and Trademark Office by International Bible Society.

Scripture references marked NKJ are taken from the New King James Version, © 1979, 1980, 1982 by Thomas Nelson, Inc., Publishers. Used by permission.

Scripture references marked NASB are taken from the New American Standard Bible, © 1960, 1963, 1968, 1971, 1972, 1973, 1975, 1977 by The Lockman Foundation. Used by permission.

ISBN 1-4141-0096-5
Library of Congress Catalog Card Number: 2003115839

"Blessed is the man who endures temptation; for when he has been approved, he will receive the crown of life which the Lord has promised to those who love Him."

(James 1:12 NKJ)

Contents

Foreword 9

Acknowledgments 11

My Prayer 15

Introduction 17

Chapter One: The Secret in the Pew 21

Chapter Two: The Trap Called Porn 31

Chapter Three: Sexuality and Lust 39

Chapter Four: The Destruction of the Wife
                and Family 47

Chapter Five: Depravity 55

Chapter Six: The Ultimate Solution 63

Chapter Seven: Accountability 75

Chapter Eight: Level the Playing Field 85

Chapter Nine: Walk in the Spirit, Deny
                the Flesh 97

Chapter Ten: Keep on Pouring 107

Notes 117

Foreword

Pornography has long been a destructive element in our society but since the arrival of the Internet, it has grown to proportions that no one could have imagined. Unfortunately, it has infiltrated our churches through the lives of Christian men and it is clearly undermining the development of godly character and leadership. Pornography not only destroys the man but it is ruining marriages, families, and even churches.

In this book, David illustrates the addictive nature of pornography and its devastating effects in the lives of those who consume it. His insights come from his own experiences while living the life of a sexual addict. After many attempts to break free from this stronghold in his life and being sickened by the man that he had become, David knew his only way back was through the power of God. As he gave both his struggles and his life into God's hands, he saw a restoration that is nothing short of miraculous. Today he is an outstanding staff minister at Phoenix First Assembly and is helping others dealing with the same problem.

David is passionate about helping men to be set free from this trap. A man bound by sexual sin will never see his full potential in Christ and will forever live a defeated life. His desire is to see men strive towards and ultimately develop into their role as spiritual leaders in their homes and churches.

If you or someone you love is struggling with sexual sin, I encourage you to read this book. It is written with both practical and biblical insights and I believe it provides helpful instruction on your path to wholeness. Never forget that Jesus Christ is your only answer in this battle! I urge you to lay it at His feet and watch as the power of God transforms, restores, and renews your life into something beautiful.

—Pastor Tommy Barnett
Phoenix First Assembly of God

Acknowledgments

My most important acknowledgement is to my Lord and Savior, Jesus Christ. Thank You for loving me when I was unlovable and directing my path back to You. It is only through Your complete forgiveness, continual grace, unconditional love, and limitless power that I walk in victory. You have shown me how you can take a shameful past and use it for Your glory. You have taught me that I can do all things through You who gives me strength. Thank You for a new beginning and my blessed life.

To my wife Lisa. You are the love of my life and my very best friend. Many nights I spent in front of our computer writing this book and you never complained. Thank you for your constant encouragement and for inspiring me to be a better man. But most of all, thank you for your love and for allowing me to be your husband. It is my true honor. You are my gift from God.

To Brooke. You are not old enough to read or understand any of this, but you are my life's most special blessing. Loving you has helped me to better understand God's love for me. You are my precious baby girl and Daddy loves you more than you will ever know.

To Mom and Dad, Joyce, Charlie, Barb, and John. Thank you for being such a great example and influence throughout my life. What treasured memories I have from being loved and encouraged by all of you. How blessed I am to be a part of such a great family.

To Stan and Naomi. You give of yourselves more than any other people I know. Thank you for accepting me into your family and for all the many kind things you do for the three of us. You are loved and appreciated.

To Pastor Barnett. Every week you encourage me to stretch myself and follow through on what God has planted within me. You are an outstanding example of God working through a committed vessel. I appreciate the confidence you have shown by allowing me to be a part of your staff. Thank you for taking the time out of your busy and hectic schedule to read my manuscript and agree to write the foreword. My hope is to be another "Miracle in the House."

To Blake "Bubba" Farmer, Tom Bender, Dr. Faiz Rahman, Dr. Joseph Chavez, Dean Charlie Burns, John Knoles and everyone at Phoenix First Pastors College. Thank you for your friendship, guidance and for pouring into my life. You have all helped to mold my Christian walk and character.

To Doris Knoles. Thank you for the superb editing and all of your suggestions to make this book better. It only seemed fitting that the person who used to mark up my college papers with red ink should do my manuscript as well. Thank you!

And finally, I dedicate this book to all the Christian men whose struggle with their flesh seems insurmountable. Keep up the good fight. God has not given up on you and He is your only path to victory. I pray for you to have the courage to come clean and quit living this secret lifestyle that will ultimately destroy you. Call upon the Lord your God and allow Him to do a dramatic transformation in your life.

My Prayer

Heavenly Father, I ask that You anoint the words within this book and use them as a catalyst to help men turn their sexual struggles completely over to You.

Provide within them the courage to face sexual sin with honesty and address it with the utmost integrity.

Help them to realize that You are much greater than any stronghold upon their life and that You and You alone hold the answer to complete deliverance from sexual addiction.

I ask Father that You give them the life that they so desperately desire, free from lapses back into sexual sin. Show them Your power in a very real and personal way and give them Your peace that passes all understanding.

Draw them close to Your heart, providing love and encouragement sufficient for each and every day in their walk with You.

In Jesus' Name,
Amen

Introduction

Let's get right to the heart of the matter. If you have purchased this book or borrowed it from a friend, there is a good probability that you or someone you know is in a battle with sexual sin. There are two things you must know right off the bat: first, this battle is not exclusive to you, and secondly, you can and will come out of this battle victorious.

"How do I know this?" you may ask. I have fought the same fight. At the deepest and darkest moment of my sexual addiction, when I thought it impossible to overcome, my Deliverer and Savior, the Lord Jesus Christ had other plans. He has shown me that I can do all things through Him who gives me strength.

I have read many good books on the subjects of pornography and sexual addiction. But the one thing

I was lacking was concrete biblical and practical ways to overcome this giant that was overcoming me. God brought me through this very dark period in my life and gave me a second chance with a fresh new start and I want to share it with you.

My desire in this book is to show you that you are not beyond hope. You can live the life you desire and dream of—a life committed to God and to your spouse, free of lapses back into the sexual sin that you have become so predictably consumed with.

I am going to be very frank and personally forthcoming. I am by no means proud of where I have come from. My purpose is to let you see that if God can deliver me, He can surely deliver you. The three things I ask of you are:

1. Be honest with yourself, your spouse, and most importantly with God.
2. You must sincerely want to see a change in your behavior and lifestyle.
3. You must believe in your heart that the power of God is greater than any bondage or addiction in your life.

I have been where you are. I know how worthless you feel. I know that you feel like God can never forgive you. Time and time again you have asked for forgiveness, but in a day or two, you have gone right back into the fire. The thing you need to remember is that God will forgive you no matter what you have done. He loves you unconditionally, no matter what condition you are in. His desire is to free you of these chains that bind you. God's freedom will help you focus on the most important issues in life: your relationship with Him and your family.

The main problem is that sex and all those things related to it have become your god. You worship at that altar more than any other. You have relegated God way down on the priority scale. Is it a wonder that you cannot overcome? It's because you are trying to do it all in your own strength. You say, "I got myself into this mess and I can get myself out." Nice theory Einstein, but it won't work. Your fascination with porn and sexual gratification has exceeded your appetite for God. That, my friend, is the problem.

Ephesians 6:12 says: *"For we do not wrestle against flesh and blood, but against principalities, against powers, against the rulers of the darkness of this age, against spiritual hosts of wickedness in the heavenly places"* (NKJ). Believe me when I tell you that pornography and sexual immorality come from the supreme ruler of darkness. It is but one more device to draw man away from serving God. So I ask you, why then would you go into a spiritual battle and not call on the name of the only One who can bring you out in one piece? If you refuse to turn this battle completely over to God, you will never see victory.

In this book, I hope to give you some very clear instruction on how to overcome in this battle for your very soul. The solution is quite simple and you have all the weaponry that you need at your disposal. You have simply forgotten about them. My goal is to remind you of the promise in God's Word that you can indeed be "more than a conqueror."

CHAPTER ONE

The Secret in the Pew

There are secrets sitting in the pews of our churches throughout America. This secret is a hidden lifestyle of sexual preoccupation and perversion within the lives of Christian men. It is fueled by regular consumption of one of the most destructive forces of our time-pornography.

Pornography is a cancer in our society that has reached terminal status. Porn creates within men abnormal and unrealistic expectations of women. It produces twisted attitudes and reduces them to nothing more than a sexual object. Porn has long been a major contributor in destroying fidelity within the covenant of marriage. A natural by-product of regular consumption of pornography in a man is an inability to maintain an intimate and loving relationship with his wife as set forth by God. Porn also reaches into the realm of single men who are doomed for relational failure even before they begin.

Many problems that couples experience with regard to intimacy, self-esteem, sexual expectations, and sexual fulfillment can be directly traced to involvement with pornography. The statistics on pornography are staggering, the availability is endless, and the results of continued use and exposure are devastating.

I know just how devastating this addiction can be. I was held within its grip for almost seven years of my life. When I finally hit rock bottom, I didn't even recognize the man I had become. How could I have degenerated to such a pathetic state? After all, I grew up in a Christian home and was raised by two incredible parents who taught me right from wrong and to love and fear God. I was clean cut with an above-average income and held a respectable job managing a multi-state territory. To look at me, no one would suspect that there was anything wrong with my life. I sat in the pew and was actively involved in the music department of my church. No one knew of my secret lifestyle or that I had become a full-blown sexual addict. This is the danger with porn and sexual addiction. It is a quiet and private thing. It all takes place within your own little world and unless you share it with another, no one ever really knows the depths that you have gone.

How this cancer has worked its way into our churches corrupting the very fiber of Christian men is not a mystery. The advent of the Internet has single-handedly been the greatest contributor. Now with complete anonymity and a click of a mouse, pornography is readily available in your home or office. The most disturbing thing is that we have allowed this smut to enter our lives at all, knowing full well that it is a sinful activity.

Pornography has created such a stronghold on men within the body of Christ that many have become neutralized from being any kind of force for the kingdom of God. That is exactly where the enemy wants us—to be of no threat to him and his work. We may call it a sexual addiction, when really it is simply a lack of self-control. Satan looks at it as a vulnerable area in your life and he intends to capitalize on your vulnerability to keep you down.

There are secrets sitting in the pews of your church as well. They are like I was, involved and on the surface, seeming to be living a godly life. But deep inside is a person who is out of control. These secrets may look like a devoted church member, a Sunday school teacher, a board member and yes, even a pastor. You may be one of the secrets yourself. Pornography is an equal-opportunity addiction. It does not discriminate.

This secret lifestyle of sexual immorality is shattering marriages, families, and churches. It prevents men from fulfilling their true destiny in Christ. The worst part is that this lifestyle is much more common within Christian men than you may think. This is a discouraging and unacceptable bit of truth. But for me (as if this was any consolation) it helped me realize that I wasn't the freakish exception, but instead, the more common rule.

While doing research for this book, I discovered some staggering statistics. It is estimated that the pornography industry generates over 12 billion dollars a year in revenue. To put this into perspective for you, it exceeds the combined revenue of the National Football League, National Basketball Association, and Major League Baseball.[1] One can only imagine the collective income generated from the entire sex industry, legal and illegal. The Maryland Coalition Against Pornography states that nationally there are 400 adult magazine publications; 20,000 adult bookstores with most having peep shows exhibiting the most violent and bizarre kinds of sex; and 800 adult movie theatres.[2] According to Enough is Enough, an organization devoted to protecting children and families from the dangers of porn, there are now more outlets for hard core pornography in the United Stares than McDonald's restaurants.[3]

Tim Wilkins, Director of CROSS Ministry, states there are over 200,000 pornographic web sites on the Internet with 300 new sites added every day.[1] A survey conducted by the Maryland Coalition Against Pornography concluded that 40 to 60 percent of Christian men are involved with pornography in some way.[2] That is four to six out of every ten Christian men! Promise Keepers reports that one third of the men who attended rallies in 1996 admitted to a personal struggle with pornography.[4]

Most disturbing were the results from a confidential survey conducted by Patrick Means and published in his book, *Men's Secret Wars*. This study confirmed that 64 percent of the evangelical pastors and lay leaders surveyed struggled with sexual addiction, which included pornography and other secret sexual activity. Furthermore, 14 percent admitted to having sexual contact short of intercourse and 25 percent confessed to having committed adultery. All of this occurred after becoming a Christian.[5]

We already know that pornography in the secular world is huge, but what I have learned since God delivered me from my addiction is truly unbelievable. I struggle with the fact that porn has become so prevalent within the lives of Christian men of all walks and denominations. These statistics of porn within our churches are unacceptable and a cause for great concern. My heart breaks for Christian men who, like me, allowed their desire for sexual gratification to overshadow everything else in their life including God. It is a life with no victory, bound so tightly that you think you will never be set free. It is living a lie to both your immediate family and church family.

Who are these secrets in the pews? Some are perceived as spiritual giants within their congregation when they aren't even the spiritual leader in their own home. Some are in important decision-making positions within the church while their personal decisions revolve around feeding the sexual desires raging inside. Some are elders and highly respected members who grant little respect to anyone of the opposite gender because all they can see is possible sexual conquest. This is the world of sexual addiction. It isn't pretty and it deceives all who are involved.

Viewing pornography is where it started for me. It seemed under control but like every addictive activity in life, it eventually grows and becomes more and more consuming. This is commonly referred to as the escalation of the addiction. In a nutshell, it is the inevitable by-product of sexual addiction. There is the need to attain something different, because what used to satisfy your sexual urges no longer does. Boredom sets in, breeding desires for something new and fresh, resulting in bolder actions.

Your involvement with pornography will inevitably go from visual to physical, from viewing porn on the Internet, to cyber or phone sex, to involvement at topless bars. When that doesn't do it for you anymore, it usually leads to active sexual involvement outside of the marriage. When that takes too much time and energy to cultivate, sexual favors are sought elsewhere, including a willingness to pay for them. The desire that wells up inside can no longer be satisfied through viewing photos and masturbation. Something more is needed-a bigger thrill at a higher cost. Greater risks are taken to obtain your sexual satisfaction. This is where my addiction took me. When I came to the end of my rope, I was in credit card debt to the tune of $40,000, the majority of which was from repeated cash advances to pay for sexual activity and maintain an addictive lifestyle that I couldn't possibly afford.

The Secret in the Pew

It wasn't the mounting debt that brought me to my knees. It was the realization that as hard as I tried to quit, I couldn't. Time after time after time I vowed to never go back but I did, over and over again. There was a feeling of desperation, knowing that my life was like a runaway train heading for the end of the track. It was sobering. I once was in control and lived life on my own terms. Somehow and at some time (I don't know exactly when) I became a slave to something that used to bring me temporary pleasure. But it only brought great pain and reminded me of how pathetic I had become.

For many people like me, the average day consisted of planning and fantasizing over what I would do to quench the craving inside. I went through the motions at work and did just what was required to maintain my position and then I raced off somewhere. Perhaps it was to the video store, the topless bar, the nude modeling studio, the massage parlor, or perhaps to seek out a prostitute. I did my dirty deed and went home, guilt ridden, convincing myself that this was the last time. And at that moment, I found a little solace and moved on. I was living a lie, to my family and to my Creator. The outward appearance presented one who had it all together. But if someone could have looked inside, they would have seen a man torn apart and void of any real happiness or contentment.

My purpose for writing this book is simple. I am tired of the stronghold that Satan has upon men in our churches. If we ever hope to live a victorious

Christian life and be the spiritual leader in our homes, we must rid our life of sexual sin. This problem, if not addressed, can and will destroy your life as you know it. Thousands of Christian men have settled for living a defeated life full of despair and hopelessness. These are all by-products of a serious sexual addiction.

Gentlemen, we are called to a higher level in Christ Jesus. We are called to be the head of our household, the Christ-like example, and the visual and guiding influence for our wives and our children. We will never fulfill that role if our heart and mind are bound by something as devastating as pornography. Satan is using this form of temptation to destroy your relationship with God, and to ruin any victory or testimony that you may have for Jesus. His plan is to make you feel unworthy and defeated at all times so that you will no longer be any threat to him. When this occurs, his plan has succeeded.

My hope is that after reading this book, you will realize the path you have embarked on will ultimately reap destruction. Please don't go to the levels that I did before you cry out to God for deliverance from this lifestyle. My story is an all-too-common one and is being experienced by men within the church all over this country. Sadly, many will never turn this over to God. They will continue to live a miserable existence as a sexual addict. Please don't let this be you. I pray that you will take the necessary steps to be honest and identify your problem, lay it at the feet of Jesus, and submerge your-self in the most important of all relationships, serving God with all of your heart, mind, soul, and spirit.

CHAPTER TWO

The Trap Called Porn

"With persuasive words she led him astray; she seduced him with her smooth talk. All at once he followed her like an ox going to the slaughter, like a deer stepping into a noose till an arrow pierces his liver, like a bird darting into a snare, little knowing it will cost him his life."

(Proverbs 7:21–23 NIV)

I am going to use the terms porn addiction, sexual addiction, sexual sin, and the like as words to describe the problems that you are facing right now. You see, they are all one and the same. You can call it what you may, and you can even give it different degrees of severity, but it all boils down to the fact that you cannot control your behavior. The truth is, your sexual urges are controlling you. This is also combined with the fact that you are in the biggest spiritual battle of your life. As I mentioned in the introduction, pornography is just one of many vices that Satan uses to keep you away from serving God.

You probably started like most of us, viewing some occasional porn in a magazine, or on the Internet, or on an X-rated video. Soon the viewing became more frequent and 99.9 percent of the time, masturbation was involved. You excused away the guilt by saying, "I am a man, and I have my needs." For some weird reason, men think it is some kind of masculine right of passage to indulge ourselves in this way and consider it acceptable behavior.

What seemed innocent and of no harm in the beginning has already created two problems for you. The first problem is that you have introduced adrenaline into your sexual identity or fiber. I can probably best describe it by the following illustration. My psychology professor told a story of a colleague that had counseled a man who had frequent pre-marital sex with his girlfriend, who later became his wife. Because the sex occurred in the back seat of his car, there was a real and constant fear of getting caught by the police or other motorists who might drive into the area where they parked. Adrenaline became a normal part of his sexual activity. The problem surfaced on his wedding night. Every time he and his wife would attempt to make love, he couldn't perform sexually. The solution was that they continued to have sex in the back seat of their car. It was the only thing that would work because sex void of the expected adrenaline rush he had become conditioned to, did not even arouse him. The counseling was an attempt to find a solution to this major problem in their marriage.

Now back to your viewing of pornography. You know that masturbating over these sexual images is wrong. This creates conviction and worry deep inside and you fear getting caught. So here you are, performing this act of arousal with yourself. But at the same time, you are desperately hoping not to get caught in the act by your parents or room mate (if you are single) or by your spouse (if you are married). What happens is simple: your mind relates ejaculation with adrenaline. It doesn't sound like a big problem, but it is, and you too have introduced adrenaline into your sexual activity just like the man in my illustration. This adrenaline factor increases as your activities get bolder and more daring. With some individuals who get involved with prostitution and other illegal acts, this adrenaline issue can render a man incapable of not just performing sexually, but also incapable of even desiring to perform sexually under normal conditions.

For you who are married, normal sexual relations with your wife is relaxed and without that adrenaline rush you have become accustomed to. You have programmed your body so that if adrenaline is not present, there is a lack of desire, satisfaction, and fulfillment. Now you no longer desire to have sexual relations with the one you love. So you avoid sexual encounters with your spouse out of fear that she will know something is wrong with you and your cover will be blown. So where does it take you? Back to porn where you can be fulfilled and fantasize over a nameless image. It is simple, uncomplicated and on your own terms.

There is a second huge problem with viewing pornography and masturbating. During this period of sexual arousal, your brain releases an adrenal gland hormone called epinephrine. This chemical goes right into the memory center of your brain where these pornographic images you have been fantasizing over become locked in just like a Kodak moment.[1] That negative is always on file and almost impossible to delete from your memory. These images come back time and time again. The more porn you view, the more frequently this happens. Soon you spend most of your time is reliving the memory of these images and remembering the physical pleasure of the ejaculation that was experienced. Now you are aroused and you want to go right back and do the same thing all over again. This is the trap called porn.

I liken this trap to a spider's web. It is sticky and you cannot pull yourself loose. You lay in the web until either the spider comes to devour you, or you just simply die a slow agonizing death of starvation and separation. You may ask, "What do you mean by devour?" Let me explain. Your little porn addiction, which seemed to start as nothing big, will continue to escalate. Like any addiction, you want something more.

Viewing photos in a magazine or on the Internet becomes boring and simply unfulfilling. Your desires and fantasies change from viewing still photos and videos to wanting to see and interact with a real live person. Commonly, men develop a secret lifestyle of visiting places where flesh is peddled: strip clubs, sex clubs, and private modeling establishments. You soon become tired of being just an observer and become obsessed with wanting physical sexual activity. Often men will start to patronize massage parlors where extra amounts of money combined with shrewd negotiations can provide certain sexual favors. As always, you are left wanting more as the hunger and desire continues to grow within. Eventually, you break the law, spend outrageous sums of money, and hire an escort so that you can have full-blown sexual intercourse.

When the costs of such a lifestyle becomes prohibitively expensive, you become willing to seek out the street prostitute. Due to your lust-driven condition and lack of thinking straight, you completely overlook the real dangers involved with this activity. She could very well be an addict so desperate for money your physical well-being could be in jeopardy. Or perhaps she is a carrier of the HIV virus. You become willing to risk your health or life and even time in jail if caught. Some men will develop perversions and desire even more twisted activities such as frequenting swingers clubs where they can have multiple partners and orgies. Some are willing to pay to be sexually dominated and humiliated.

Others experiment and delve into homosexuality. Most sad of all are those who develop and perpetrate violent behavior from sexual assault to rape and even child molestation.

Many of you have gone to some of these levels, and some of you who are just starting out are thinking that this can never happen to you. This is where you are dead wrong. Escalation of the addiction happens to everyone and it happened to me. I minister to men who have gone down this path. They tell me unbelievable stories of where their sexual addiction took them. Generally, it takes us to the end of the rope. That time comes when you realize that you are so far out of control that you never dreamed you could be doing some of the things you are doing.

You spend most of your waking hours dwelling on what you are going to do that day to feed the sexual desire inside. You are financially ruined trying to keep up with your habits. Your productivity at work has eroded. Your relationship with your wife or family is non-existent. And you are so far away from God that He becomes nothing more than a swear word you hear spoken occasionally. This is what I mean by being devoured.

The starvation and separation I mentioned is your self-imposed seclusion. You want nothing to do with those who love you, only those who wish to slowly destroy you and take your money. You are so starved from natural forms of affection, that you can't even remember what they are. You have replaced them with unnatural forms that will never satisfy. You have gone on a hunger strike from God because you really believe He can no longer love you in your current pathetic state. So you start to die a little every day. You feel so worthless that you sometimes wish you were dead. You feel helpless to make a change because you have tried many times before and were unsuccessful.

This isn't a pretty picture, but you need to know what pornography does to a man. Do not think that you are above this happening to you. It happened to me. It is happening with regularity to well-respected men from every walk of life. Unfortunately, it is reaching epidemic proportions. My sincere desire is for you get control of this problem before it completely controls you.

CHAPTER THREE

Sexuality and Lust

"Flee sexual immorality. All other sins a man commits are outside his body, but he who sins sexually sins against his own body. Do you not know that your body is the temple of the Holy Spirit, who is in you, whom you have received from God? You are not your own; you were bought at a price. Therefore honor God with your body."

(1 Corinthians 6:18–20 NIV)

Let's start by understanding that our sex drive and sexuality is a gift from God. It is nothing to be ashamed of and certainly nothing to fear. I once heard Chuck Swindoll on the radio tell a story about Adam. After God had brought all of the animals to him to be named, He could see that Adam was lonely and realized that he needed a mate. So God put Adam into a deep sleep, took one of his ribs, and formed Eve. When God brought Eve to Adam and said, "Adam, what shall you call her?" Adam responded, WHOA-MAAAN!!

God knew exactly what He was doing when He created woman. He knew that her body, so different from ours, would be a beautiful thing to behold. After everything that I have personally gone through with regard to pornography and sexual addiction, and having been delivered from its grip, I still don't think there is anything more attractive, alluring, or beautiful than the mate that God created for me. You see, I didn't ask God to take away my sexual desire or drive, I asked Him to help me keep it in check and in the proper context. Now my desires are focused and aimed at the love of my life, my wife Lisa. No longer do I need to go elsewhere for sexual gratification. God has given me everything I need to be completely fulfilled in her.

Satan has taken this God-given drive and has perverted and counterfeited it just like he does everything else. We have been drawn into the lie that there is something more out there, something that is unattainable within the realm of marriage. We are told that sex within the confines of marriage is boring and unfulfilling. We want something more daring, more provocative, and more twisted.

We dream of this porn queen who we believe to be a nymphomaniac, a sex machine made exclusively for our personal delight, looking straight at me with passion in her eyes and desiring only me. What a joke! We never seem to recognize that she is also caught in a trap. I am convinced that if you asked any woman involved in the sex industry, she would say that she never dreamed as a young girl that this would be a way of life for her. They too, have bought into the lies of the enemy. For a season they will enjoy their celebrity status and reap great financial rewards but in time, they will age and be discarded like yesterdays news by the pornography industry. The truth is, to her you are simply a means to an end. She is more than likely sickened by you and the many other men who have come before you who she views as desperate and perverted.

Why do we imagine such unrealistic and foolish things while viewing these pornographic images as mentioned above? Because of fantasy. In our twisted minds we conjure up all kinds of scenarios during this fantasy process, and we actually start to believe them. The fact is, some guys spend more time fantasizing about sexual scenarios than acting upon them. Some will eventually lose their jobs when the escalation of the addiction progresses. This is because they become so gripped with the fantasy that they cannot function in the realm of reality. Then you walk around very much like a preoccupied zombie with little motivation or care. You become a shell of the man you once were and your only desire is seeking a fix for the lust that has welled up inside of you. All of your attention and energy evolves around sex, not family, not God, just sex. This is a terrible place to be and unfortunately most of those who come to this point aren't even aware that they have arrived.

Some of you reading this are a living testament to this reality. Others are well on their way. This is consistent with sexual addiction as it develops and starts to take on a life of its own. *"But each one is tempted when he is carried away and enticed by his own lust. Then when lust has conceived, it gives birth to sin; and when sin is accomplished, it brings forth death. Do not be deceived, my beloved brethren"* (James 1:14–16 NASB).

The major obstacle is overcoming our lust. We make conscious decisions every day regarding lust. It reminds me of the fight-or-flight syndrome. When cornered and in danger do we stand there and fight our way out, or do we flee? It depends on your own personal conditioning. Reaction to lust is the same. Am I going to purge the lustful thoughts from my mind or am I going to entertain them? If I choose to entertain them, it will surely lead to sin. That is what Satan wants us to do. *"You have heard that it was said, 'Do not commit adultery.' But I tell you that any-one who looks at a woman lustfully has already com-mitted adultery with her in his heart"* (Matthew 5:27–28 NIV). I guess that pretty much spells it out for us. Entertaining lustful thoughts is a sin, and so there-fore we need to do everything we can to flush them from our mind.

A good friend and my former Bible college pro-fessor said it in a very simple way, "You can let a bird fly over your head, just don't let him nest in your hair." In other words, it is not a sin unless and until you dwell and fantasize on it. When that lady at the mall walks by who has purposefully dressed provocatively to capture the looks and stares of men, it is ok to recognize her. But please, don't twist your neck around like a contortionist and watch every movement of her body. Quit thinking what it would be like to see her naked or fantasize about a sexual encounter with her. That is when it becomes sin.

It is what you choose to do with the thoughts and images that enter your mind that will start or put an end to the lust process. You can in fact, stop lust and fantasy long before they begin. With God's help you can condition yourself to refuse to let this process start. One area that continued to haunt me and most other men who have stopped their involvement with pornography is remembering the past. Memories and images you had experienced before can pop back into your head without warning at any time. If you are not careful you can start to relive those experiences in your mind. This is, as my friend said, allowing that bird to nest. You cannot let this happen.

Long after God delivered me from my insatiable desire for every possible form of adult entertainment (as they call it); I could be driving in my car and out of the blue would come a vivid memory. I would say in my mind, "Lord, where did that come from?" knowing full well the source. I would automatically speak audibly in my car. "Satan, I rebuke you in the name of Jesus. I am a child of the Most High God and greater is He who is in me, than anything you can bring my way. I am washed by the precious blood of Jesus Christ and you have no power or authority over me. Get out of my car, in the name of JESUS!" When you speak forth the name of Jesus, the devil has to flee and does every time. The name of Jesus has power over Satan.

My pastor was speaking one Sunday about his early days in Phoenix. He was in the beginning stages of a building program. The church had enough money to buy the property and dig the foundations, and then the funds were dry. As they were working with the banks about funding the project, Satan was doing everything in his power to discourage my pastor. Satan was putting doubt in his mind about the decisions that were made, and the ability to even obtain the funding that was required. He was driving by the project when Satan was giving him a ration of negative, discouraging thoughts. Pastor said that he could hear these words in his mind, "You are going to be the laughing stock of Phoenix. Look, all you have is this big hole and now you can't even finish what you started. You are a big loser and this only proves it!"

My pastor went one step further from my form of rebuking Satan. He spoke forth the name of Jesus and put the devil in his place. Then he pulled the car off of the road, got out and walked over to the passenger side, opened the door and yelled, "NOW GET OUT AND DON'T COME BACK!" Needless to say, the church got built and is now one of the largest and greatest soul-winning churches in the United States.

Sexuality and Lust

There is POWER in the name of Jesus and in the Word of God. Men, you need to memorize scripture and speak it out during times of temptation. These Words of Life can stop dead in its tracks any thought, lust or temptation. When you fill yourself with God's Word, it is like ammunition, ready to shoot down the enemy. When you know how to deflect the fiery arrows that Satan sends your way, you will begin to live a life free of sexual sin. It is all about shutting it down before it begins. Many men are proving this can be accomplished since they got serious about their problem and most importantly, in their relationship with God.

I want to go back to the point that I made about the sexual images that kept coming back to haunt me time and time again. I know that these images were seared into my brain throughout the many years of my deep involvement in porn and many other sexually addictive activities. What I want you to know is that after God did a work in my life, I started to address another issue with Him. I asked God to purge my mind of these images and memories that would pop back into my mind without an invitation. I am here to tell you that God has performed another great miracle in my life. It is now a rare event. In fact, I can't even tell you when the last time a pornographic memory has entered my mind. If you knew where I had come from, you would understand exactly how miraculous that is! God has accomplished things in my life that the experts say cannot be done. He has deleted the memory banks in my mind that were once overflowing with nothing but filthy reminders of my past life.

God continues to do a work in me. I am so thankful to Him that He has given my life back to me. This is the reason I call this a process, because to me it was and continues to be. When you get serious with God, He will get serious with you. Everything you need, He has to offer. Victory in this fight is attainable, but not until you allow God to do a work in your life.

CHAPTER FOUR

The Destruction of the Wife and Family

"Let your fountain be blessed, and rejoice with the wife of your youth. As a loving deer and graceful doe, let her breasts satisfy you at all times; and always be enraptured with her love. For why should you, my son, be enraptured by an immoral woman, and be embraced in the arms of a seductress?"
(Proverbs 5:18–20 NKJ)

The secret life you are living has many casual ties. We already know that the man engaged in this lifestyle suffers greatly because he is miserable in his marriage, his Christian walk, his profession, and every other aspect of his life. His wife suffers in silence, never fully understanding what has gone wrong and feeling utterly helpless in correcting it. She simply wants her husband back, that loving and giving man she married. She is starving for some genuine affection and love from him, but it cannot happen because his desire is for an unnamed image he carries around in his mind.

You may say, "I have not had an affair, I have been faithful to my wife." My response would be, "Who are you kidding?" Just because you haven't taken your addiction to physical involvement with another women does not make you faithful. You crossed that line a long time ago when you allowed yourself to have an affair of the mind. These images that you continually view are the objects of your fantasy and affection. They have become your most-sought-after treasure. You fantasize about imaginary sexual encounters with these nameless sex goddesses whose sole purpose is to grant you complete sexual gratification.

Then you look at your wife and say to yourself, "Why can't she look like that centerfold model?" The truth is that no one does. These women, many of whom have had their bodies further perfected by surgery and whose images have been computer enhanced, just don't exist in the real world. Have you looked at yourself lately? Why don't you look like some of the men in the fitness magazines with the six-pack stomachs and two-percent body fat? We hold our spouses to an impossible standard. If we were held to the same standard we too would surely fail.

Your continued involvement with pornography will ultimately destroy your marriage and family. It slowly chips away at the very foundation of the union between a husband and wife. Thomas Parker says, "There are few dangers to the sanctity of this divinely ordained institution [marriage] that exceed the threat of porn. It is here that the holy communion of the sexual relationship between a husband and wife is trivialized. Porn attacks the concepts of love, affection, contentment, and fidelity. In fact it despises them, and it literally teaches contempt for the very glue that holds the marriage and family together. There is no longer any connection between sex and families, between sex and love, between sex and commitment."[9]

A study conducted by Indiana University's Dolph Zillman and University of Houston colleague Jennings Bryant concluded the following: Exposure to massive amounts of soft-core pornography develops sexual dissatisfaction in both genders, particularly men. When comparing their spouse's response to sexual behavior portrayed in pornographic materials, both men and women became dissatisfied with their spouse's sexual performance. Dissatisfaction with the physical appearance of their intimate partners was evident as well. They even found their partners less attractive and even less worthy individuals.[10]

This is the problem that porn creates—unrealistic expectations of our spouse and sex. It acts to distort your image of your wife and how she should perform sexually. Now, nothing that your wife does satisfies you. You become even more critical of her body and your sex life. Over time, you find that you start to look at all women, including those who you work with, as nothing more than a potential sexual partner. This is the mindset that pornography creates. Before you began consuming porn, making love to your wife was satisfying and you could actually work with a woman in a professional setting without thinking of her in a sexual light.

We have taken sexual intercourse, with all of the intimacy and love that God intended it to encompass, and have turned it into an act. It becomes an activity that we have designed for our own personal pleasure. Many men wonder why sex is non-existent in their marriage and even use it as the excuse for their activity with pornography. The truth is that when you stopped giving while making love with your wife, things started to fall apart. Why would any woman want to give herself to a man who is in it for one thing, his own sexual pleasure and release? That is not what making love is all about. It is about a union between a husband and wife. The joining of body, soul, and spirit. It is about mutual fulfillment and the giving of yourself to the one you love and have committed your life to.

The truth is, not only are you having sex for your own personal gratification, but you are also thinking of another woman while being with your wife. Those pornographic images and sexual experiences of yours have been seared into your brain. Now you can't think of anything else because of the pollution of your mind. Your wife has become relegated to a piece of meat, a warm body, a lover by proxy. Intimacy has now become nonexistent and your wife knows this all too well. So not only are you not giving to your partner, you are not even with your partner.

Probably the most powerful question I ask when I speak to men's groups on this topic is, "How would you feel if you knew the exact moment of conception of your child and realized that you were thinking of another woman?" Think about it! It is a sobering and sickening thought. How many times have you made love to your wife and mentally been with another?

This is not your wife's fault. You have created the problem and she is the one who is paying the greatest price. Do you have any idea of the pain and humiliation that you are putting her through? If you only knew how much you have hurt her, and if you still truly care for her, it would be enough for you to stop your involvement with porn.

When I have spoken at churches, I have had women approach me and ask if I could talk with their husbands about this issue. The hurt and rejection they experience is sometimes insurmountable. They feel unloved, betrayed, used, and like a forgotten friend. They are broken, without hope.

You have developed this hopelessness within her because your heart is with another. You are to blame. It may not bother you where your life is heading. But please, wake up and realize that your addiction is affecting more people than you think. The ones who are paying the highest toll are the very ones you love the most—your wife and your children.

You are even underestimating the ability of your kids to read between the lines. Children sense when a marriage has lost its intimacy. They are not stupid. They wonder why Dad and Mom spend so much time apart. They wonder why their dad doesn't show affection to their mother. They feel like they are living with two roommates who love them but question if they truly love each other.

Men, you are developing within your own sons an attitude towards women that will greatly affect their ability to maintain a relationship with a woman they love. Your son is watching you. You are his role model. And though you may not be willing at this point to change your ways, might you do so for your son? Do not let him continue down the path that you have started.

Show your children what being a man is all about! Love your wife like you love yourself. I cannot think of a better gift to give your children than being an example of a Godly man. Put your family first, and love your wife and children so completely that they will better understand their heavenly Father's love. This will help your children to develop and maintain a relationship with someone of the opposite sex and keep it within a godly context both before and after marriage. This is a standard that you can pass on to them only if you purge your life of this menace and fill it with intimacy with God.

Don't let your pride get in the way. Pride is a major reason why men do not seek help with sexual addiction. We want to believe we can do it on our own. We are ashamed to let someone else know that we are flawed. You are not perfect. Welcome to the real world! We all have problems and areas that we struggle with. But if we don't allow God to eliminate the porn problem, it will cause destruction in the life of our families.

CHAPTER FIVE

Depravity

"Furthermore, since they did not think it worth-while to retain the knowledge of God, he gave them over to a depraved mind, to do what ought not to be done."

(Romans 1:28 NIV)

This is a chapter that wasn't originally planned for this book. In fact, I thought I had completed this project. But for weeks, Romans 1:18–32 started to resonate in my mind. Now I cannot conclude this book without discussing this issue. I believe God has purposely laid this upon my heart to show you what can develop in average men who lose control of their own sexual drives and identity.

The recent deluge of news stories over the past several months of child abductions, rape, and murder triggered this issue. There are more than I could ever remember in the past. They are disgusting tales of precious little girls from five to seven years of age being abducted and violated sexually before they are systematically murdered. Then there are stories of teenage girls being brutally raped, beaten, or killed. It is downright sickening.

There is the terrible story of seven-year-old Danielle Van Dam of San Diego who was raped and murdered by her own neighbor who lived two doors down. Her convicted killer, David Westerfield, was a 50-year-old design engineer. Prosecutors say he kidnapped and murdered Danielle because he harbored sexual fantasies about young girls. He was also in possession of child pornography found on his computers.

Leesa Marie Gray, a sixteen-year-old from Mississippi, was kidnapped, savagely raped, tortured, and strangled by a customer who visited the restaurant where she worked. The convicted perpetrator, Gunnery Sgt. Thomas "Eddie" Loden, a Marine recruiter lay in wait for Leesa to leave work that evening in June. Not only did Loden commit such horrible acts, but a videotape was found in a camcorder located in his van. I assume this was so he could re-live his unfathomable act of brutality and serve as a trophy for his actions. Also found in his van stuffed under the back seat, was Leesa's lifeless body. Loden was a husband and a father of a young daughter with no criminal record. Investigators found a large assortment of hard core pornography at his home and Internet logs on his home computer showing visits to web sites that explained how to rape a teenage girl and others promoting sex between fathers and daughters. His former wife stated that he had an unquenchable thirst for porn and sexual perversion.

Five-year-old Samantha Runnion of Stanton, California, was snatched from her own front yard. According to witnesses, the suspect asked Samantha to help him find his lost dog. When she agreed to help, he grabbed her and threw her into a car while she kicked and screamed for help. When Samantha's little body was found, she had been raped, bruised, and asphyxiated. Her accused murderer, Alejandro Avila, a 27-year-old production line supervisor at a medical equipment plant, had been acquitted on previous molestation charges filed two years earlier.

A story broke recently of an international child porn ring being busted with several participants living right here among us. The story says that these men allowed their own children to be filmed while being sexually abused by others to sell on the Internet. As a father, I find this news to be unconscionable as did the FBI agent who was interviewed. This is a man who has seen more than his share of violent and perverted behavior, but he still was visibly shaken by what he and other agents had uncovered. This recent explosion of events occurring throughout our nation and world has filled me with such sadness and rage that I am compelled to speak out.

What is it that can take a man from being a loving father to one who exploits his own flesh and blood for money and sexual pleasure? What can drive a man to participate in sexual activity with a precious child of God? Who can look into the innocent eyes of a small child and do such unspeakable things? What kind of a human being can even consider acting out such atrocities as these? How can a mind become so cold and twisted?

I think the greater question is: At what point does a man turn his sexual desires and fantasies from a woman to a child? Where along the road of life did this occur and what motivated him? In many if not all of these instances where you read of children being molested, raped, and murdered, you find that pornography plays a role in the life of the perpetrator. I have never interviewed these men but I am certain that pornography, in general, was a way of life for them. In their search for more, child porn crossed their path. Just like adult porn put a hook in my mouth, the viewing of child porn planted a seed in their mind that later grew. I believe this is a direct result of the escalation of the addiction. If it is not stopped, it leads to a completely perverted state of mind called depravity.

Depravity is not something that happens overnight. It is developed and nurtured. It feeds from a gradual acceptance of things once thought of as incomprehensible. Now they are found as interesting, seductive, alluring, and acceptable. It is the breakdown of a God-given standard programmed into us at birth and by which we adjust our moral compass. This standard is slowly chipped away by new experiences that are more extreme and more abnormal, by viewing more aberrant materials and continually feeding our mind with a diet of filth and sexual deviance. It is pushing the envelope for a new sexual thrill and doing or acting out something that previously would never have been considered. This is exactly what the escalation of the addiction is all about. It takes men to places that they have never been before. Once that line has been crossed, it becomes normal and comfortable.

All of these men who have committed these unbelievable acts are just like you and me. The desires that rage inside of them can only be quenched now by behavior that is unfathomable to us. And now for many of you, some of your regimented and regular sexual behavior is unfathomable to others. You have slowly allowed the enemy to take a stronghold in your life and start you down the road to depravity. It can take years and years but eventually, Satan will lead you to ultimate destruction.

Am I suggesting that everyone who is addicted to porn will ultimately become a rapist or murderer? No, but it is not only possible, but proven, that pornography and sexual addiction can take you there. Do not be deceived. Just like these men in these tragic events, you are already living a lifestyle that is far from where you started. Some of you are involved in actions and habits that you can't believe, nor could your family and friends if they knew. Some of you are on the fast track to getting there.

What condition would this nation be in today without the restraining force of the Holy Spirit actively working in the lives of godly men and women? We would be living in utter chaos and anarchy. Any moral standard would be lost. You have seen footage of people looting businesses after riots and devastating storms; this is because there is no one to restrain them. They know that the law cannot prevent them from doing their criminal activity. There simply aren't enough police officers to go around. People will always become like animals when there is no order or restraint. It has been proven time and time again.

With sexual addiction being such a private and personal thing, you have no one to hold you accountable other than yourself. No one is there to tell you that you are severely off track. You rely wholly on your own efforts to restrain yourself from doing something what your flesh wants to do anyway. In other words, there is no restraint in your decision making. You slowly get involved in activities and habits that desensitize you to what is right and wrong. Unacceptable behavior and twisted sexual fantasy become the norm. Ultimately, twisted sexual fantasy develops into twisted sexual actions. This is all in the name of getting your sexual desires fulfilled.

I am confident if you asked any of the before-mentioned sexual predators what it was that drove them to do these acts of rape, torture, and murder, they couldn't even explain it to you. But I believe I can. In Romans one, God gave people over to a depraved mind and the sinful desires of their heart. All restraint was gone. The moral compass was broken and their eyes were blinded to any truth. Their minds were void of any human compassion or reason. They were determined to feed their desires no matter what the cost. Unfortunately, someone paid the ultimate price as the victim of their senseless act.

I am trying to wake you up to where you are heading. Whether you want to admit it or not, you have already taken many steps down the road to depravity as I did. My attitudes changed. My level of acceptance became wide open because the lines I once would not have crossed disappeared. My vision became blurred and my common sense became uncommon. My moral compass was broken when it came to my sexual fulfillment. I can't believe some of the places that I have been or the many partners I have had. The risks that I had taken to fulfill the lust burning inside of me seem unreal to me now.

I am ashamed of my past, but my Savior has forgiven me and erased that part of my life. His desire is to do the same thing in your life as well as the men who are mentioned in the sad stories within this chapter. There is no sin that God cannot forgive. There is no depth of depravity that God cannot bring you out of. He can heal your mind and renew your spirit. He will wash you white as snow with the blood of Jesus and continue to purify you through the Word of God. That precious Holy Spirit can be the greatest restraining force in your life, a convicting force, a voice of reason, a source of great strength. Make a determined act of your will to change your course from the road to destruction and depravity. Start your journey down a new path with a compass that is always pointing to your ultimate source of strength and power—the Lord Jesus Christ.

CHAPTER SIX

The Ultimate Solution

"Hear my cry, O God; Attend to my prayer. From the end of the earth I will cry to you, When my heart is overwhelmed; Lead me to the rock that is higher than I. For you have been a shelter for me, A strong tower from the enemy. I will abide in your tabernacle forever; I will trust in the shelter of your wings."

(Psalm 61:1–4 NKJ)

My prayer is that by now, you admit that your life is spinning out of control and that you have become consumed by sexual preoccupation. You long for a life that consistently honors God, your wife, and maintains sexual purity. You realize that as long as you struggle with this addiction, you will never realize your full potential in Christ and the plans that He has for your life. You know you have not been able to control your temptations and desires on your own. That is exactly the place where many others and I had come to. That is the place where you find that God is your only weapon in this raging war. Without God, you will never overcome this addiction. If you can't overcome this addiction, you will never fulfill that perfect destiny He has planned for only you. It all boils down to one thing: DESIRE. Is your desire for the filth that you have been consuming greater than your desire for the things of God?

It became crystal clear to me that the only way I was going to be delivered of this mammoth obstacle in my life was through a right and committed relationship with my Creator. I am convinced that if you are dealing with this addiction you have not completely sold out to God. If you are honest with yourself, you will come to the same conclusion. What do I mean by being sold out? I mean that God needs to be paramount in your life. Your decisions, desires, motives, and lifestyle must reflect that of a man who is interested in holiness. I am not talking about a theory. I am talking about a way of life.

You see, I was living a double life. I was attending church and in just enough activities to give the impression that I was a dedicated Christian. I even tried to fool myself into believing the lie. But it was my secret life that I nurtured and spent most of my waking moments developing. This not only holds true in porn addiction, but also applies to other aspects of our lives. What do we value the most? What do we spend the lion's share of our time doing? Is it making money, sports, gambling, drinking, or viewing pornographic material? The list can go on. What is it that we have replaced God with?

My favorite scripture is Romans 12:1: *"I beseech you therefore, brethren, by the mercies of God, that you present your bodies a living sacrifice, Holy, acceptable to God, which is your reasonable service. And do not be conformed to this world, but be transformed by the renewing of your mind, that you may prove what is that good and acceptable and perfect will of God"* (NKJ). The key word here is *conformed*. We have allowed ourselves to be conformed to this world and its self-serving ways. We slowly allow things to enter into our lives that, in and of themselves, do not seem like much. But over time they develop an entirely new perspective within us. We become desensitized to truth, holiness, and what is right. Our vision becomes blurred and our purpose is driven by what has become acceptable in the world's system. We completely forget that it is not this world we are living for, but we live for Christ Jesus.

We have allowed premium cable channels in our homes that show nudity, sex, vulgar profanity, sexual scenarios, and debauchery of all kinds. We pay hard-earned money to watch movies and rent videos with more of the same. We listen with curiosity to shock jocks like Howard Stern whose apparent single daily goal is to get a female guest in his studio to strip naked. While we listen, the mental fantasy starts. We listen to music with lyrics that speak filth into our mind and spirit. We have conformed to this world by allowing all of this to be a regular part of our life.

No matter how you try to slice it or dice it, if you are watching or listening to any of the above-mentioned forms of entertainment, you are not completely sold out to God. I realized that just because many of my friends, Christian and otherwise, allowed these things into their lives and homes as an acceptable practice, didn't mean that it was acceptable for me. No, I am not some kind of monk. I just realized that none of this could be a part of my life if I was going to be an effective follower of Christ. It just can't happen, no matter how hard you try to convince yourself otherwise. That is the problem with so many within the church today. We have allowed ourselves to be seduced by the world. We try to have one foot in Satan's camp and the other in God's camp. Is it any wonder that there is no victory or power to overcome these temptations in our lives?

I have learned to live by a very simple policy in regard to the things I do, the places I go, and the materials that I read and watch. I ask myself this question, "Would I be doing this if Christ was sitting here next to me?" The truth is gentlemen, He is. We just don't see Him in the flesh. It is a matter of accountability. Would you be flirting with another woman if your wife were standing next to you? Absolutely not! (Hopefully you wouldn't flirt in any case, but I use this as an illustration.) Her very presence would keep you on the straight and narrow and hold you accountable. Likewise, if Christ were visible to you all the time, looking at you with the eyes of a disappointed father, you wouldn't do most of the questionable habits that have become an acceptable part of your life.

God wants your everything, period! He is looking for men of unquestionable integrity who will stand up unashamed, and be counted among His devoted followers. When you give it all up for the most fulfilling and rewarding relationship of your life, the contentment that follows is like nothing you have ever experienced. This contentment I speak of cannot be described, only experienced. It will sustain you during times of fear, doubt, trouble, and temptation. It will offer you the strength to deny the flesh and all of its entanglements. It is an intangible, yet powerful, and priceless commodity.

Throughout the Bible, God used people from all walks and backgrounds. If measured by the world's standards, many of them were losers. They were used to accomplish God's will and work here on this earth. How did they do the things they did? Through the power of God. But this power could not be utilized without a committed and willing vessel. These men of great courage and accomplishment had one thing in common: they completely trusted and devoted their lives to God. When this happens the results are powerful and supernatural.

God is not asking you to build an ark or set the children of Israel free from captivity. He has not asked you to call down fire from heaven or defeat a whole army with just 300 men. What He has called you to is a life of holiness. *"But as He who called you is holy, you also be holy in all your conduct, because it is written, 'Be holy, for I am holy'"* (1 Peter 1:15–16 NKJ). He asks that you serve Him with your life, your time, and your finances. He has called you to seek first the kingdom of God and His righteousness, and to love Him above everything else. It is so simple, yet we make it so complicated. God knows that His power at work in your life is greater than anything you may encounter. And that includes a sexual drive that has gone astray. To us it seems insurmountable, but it is a small order for God.

I have read many books on pornography and sexual addiction. Many of them contain outstanding information and insights to overcome this battle raging in your life. Some are authors with doctorates; others are highly educated men who delve into the psychological and physiological reasons for this problem. My conclusion has and will continue to be that the only way you will overcome this problem that is slowly destroying you is through the power of God.

I hope I have not let you down in my conclusion and solution. If I have however, it is because you have never allowed yourself to experience that life-changing, mind-altering, power-producing, relationship with Jesus Christ. Take it from an average guy who has experienced the life-changing power of God in a personal way. God cleaned me up and turned me around and gave me a power that can stand up against anything the enemy may send my way. All you need to do is seek Him with an expectant heart. Know that He is your source and develop an intimate relationship with Him. Romans 12:1 says: *"But be transformed by the renewing of your mind."* Feed yourself on the Word of God and allow your spirit to be cleansed by it. Learn about the promises and truth within the scriptures. Stand on those promises and claim them for your very own. There is power in the Word of God. All you need to do is read it and hide it in your heart.

I realize that this is a simple approach to a huge problem, but we need not make it difficult because it isn't. It is basic, easy to understand, and garners fantastic results. The question is, are you willing to give it all up for Christ? If your answer is yes, your deliverance from sexual addiction is on its way. If on the other hand you just can't give it all to Him, I am afraid you have a long road ahead. Understand this, with you it may be sexual addiction, with another it is gambling or alcohol or drugs. It is all one and the same, a distraction to prevent you from serving God. Satan has found your weakness and has capitalized on it. While doing this he has even convinced you that you cannot be delivered from what is binding you. This is just one more lie from the father of lies.

When will you learn that with God all things are possible? What will it take for you decide that enough is enough? Will it take losing it all? The casualties of a sexual addiction are many and very costly. Do not allow yourself to let this continue for another day. You need to drive a stake in the ground and say, "Today is a turning point in my life and in my relationship with God."

David's prayer of confession after he sinned with Bathsheba was: *"The sacrifices of God are a broken spirit, a broken and a contrite heart—These, O God, you will not despise"* (Psalm 51:17 NKJ). When you come to the point of being sick of your lifestyle and are broken in spirit and have humbled your heart, God will do a work in your life. That is when you come to realize that within your own strength, you are helpless and you are acknowledging that you need God to deliver you from your addiction.

I encourage you to go to your pastor or a friend who loves and cares for you. Confess your problem first to him, then go to the Lord together in sincere and earnest prayer. Ask Him to forgive you of the life you have been living and the sin you have been regularly involved with. David continues praying: *"Create in me a clean heart, O God, and renew a steadfast spirit within me"* (Psalm 51:10 NKJ). Ask God to clean up your thought process and your mind from the smut that you have been devouring for years. Ask Him to help you overcome the temptations in your life and give you a supernatural strength through the power of the Holy Spirit. Then and only then will you see a change in your life. With each small victory in the battle of overcoming sexual temptation, you will be further encouraged and strengthened. Soon after the many small victories in battle, the large victory of the war will be won.

The Ultimate Solution

This is generally a process that takes time, commitment, and a steadfast desire to seek God daily in prayer and in the Word. I have heard of some that speak of a supernatural overnight deliverance, much like you occasionally hear with a testimony from someone addicted to drugs and alcohol. This has happened, but my experience, and the experience of most of the men to whom I minister, is that it has been a process. In my life I am glad that it was a process, because I cherish my new life even more. Each victory gained showed me that with the power of the Holy Spirit working in me, I could overcome temptation. That was a constant encouragement to me. If during this time of renewal you stumble, pick yourself back up. Don't let a setback take you off course. Stay focused on God and know that He loves you and wants nothing more than to see you with complete victory in your walk with Him.

I want to share something that you need to hear about God's love. I know that at times you feel worthless, dirty, and unlovable. You even question if God is willing to forgive you, because you have asked time and time again. You have even gone as far as to make numerous promises to God. You have told Him that if He will forgive you of this transgression, you will never go back. But you went back and did it again and again. I can relate because I have been there. After a while you don't even think that He is listening any more. That is another lie from the enemy that he wants you to believe. Many of you have bought into it just like I did.

I thought I understood God's love, because I witnessed it time and time again during the process of deliverance from this addiction. His forgiveness, grace, power, and love were essential components to my deliverance. I have been completely free from this addiction for over seven years with no setbacks whatsoever. I praise God and give Him the glory!

It wasn't until Lisa and I had our first child in April of 2001 that I really started to understand the love that God has for me. I never knew that you could love something as much as I love my little baby girl. I know that I would do anything to protect her and to provide for her every need. I know that no matter what that child does, I will love her unconditionally. I hurt when she hurts and I am happy when I know that she is happy. I live to come home from work and see her smile and reach out for me to hold her. There isn't anything I would not do for my child, and God forbid if any disease would ever attack her little body. I would, without hesitation, take that disease upon myself if I could to free her from it. I know without a doubt that I would die for her. That is a father's love and it was foreign to me until the birth of our daughter. It is powerful, consuming, and unconditional. I realized that if I could love my child this much, how much more does my heavenly Father love me?

The answer is simple. We cannot comprehend in our human capabilities the love that God holds for each of us. He sent His sinless Son to this earth to die an excruciating death on a cross. This method of torture and execution was reserved for the most vile criminals. But He bore our sins so that we could be forgiven from the sexual sin that has bound us for much too long.

I know He had me and you on His mind while hanging on that cross. He took upon himself every sin—past, present, and future—so that we may live eternally with Him after this vapor of life we live on earth is done. Imagine, all you fathers, giving up your son's or daughter's life to save people who were unworthy and unappreciative. I know that is something I could never do. This is what separates God's love from ours.

His heart breaks when He knows that one of His children is not living in complete victory, especially when He gave us a road map through His example and through the Word of God. He has given us everything we need to overcome. We just need to believe it and move out of the way so that He can take over.

How much longer do you want to break the heart of your heavenly Father? Your life is slipping away. With each passing year of being controlled by your sexual desires, you die just a little more. Take this problem to God today. Ask Him to forgive you. Commit your life wholly to Him and stand strong in His power. You will no longer be controlled by your fantasy life, but instead you will be victorious in your daily spiritual walk with our Lord and Savior.

CHAPTER SEVEN

Accountability

"As iron sharpens iron, so one man sharpens another."
(Proverbs 27:17 NIV)

Men, we are an interesting breed. We seldom share our deepest, darkest secrets and difficulties with anyone. This need we feel—to be perceived as in control, strong and without a care—is something that has been portrayed to us as normal from other men in our lives. Perhaps it was your grandfather or father, or someone who greatly influenced your life as a male role model. We have all heard these statements: "Come on, take it like a man." "You need to be strong." "Don't let them see you cry." "Get out there and let them know who's the boss."

These statements resonate in our minds. Each served a purpose at a particular time; they may have served as one of those defining moments in your life to establish your manhood. This established our overall belief that we, as men, can't afford to show any weakness in life.

An old Simon and Garfunkel song says, "I am a rock, I am an island." This could never be more true. We close ourselves off from the people who care for us and could probably help if we would only share some of our struggles with them. We take this macho mentality and apply it to everything in our life—our relationships, profession, extracurricular activities and even in dealing with our most troubling issues. We simply keep it in or "suck it up" as we have often been told. We carry it around for fear of being perceived as less than a man or downright weak. Instead of addressing the problem, we just simply get deeper and deeper into it, and eventually accept it as a permanent lifestyle dysfunction. We think we can handle it, because after all, we haven't shared it with a soul. It is my personal problem and I will just have to take it like a man.

This mentality or concept of dealing with problems is the worst possible path to take when it comes to sexual addiction. It is wrong for two very simple reasons. First, when we keep our secret lifestyle hidden and known only to ourselves, it keeps us in bondage. There is something liberating, a sense of being released from a life sentence, that occurs when you make your struggles known to another. A brother in Christ can help to carry your burden and help lighten your load. *"Brothers, if someone is caught in a sin, you who are spiritual should restore him gently. But watch yourself, or you also may be tempted. Carry each other's burdens, and in this way you will fulfill the law of Christ"* (Galatians 6:1–2 NIV).

Secondly, when we don't share our problems with other believers in Christ, there is no one else to hold yourself and your actions accountable to. I am aware that ultimately, we are all responsible for our own actions and we will be held accountable to God for them. But until now, this method has not really done a thing for you in your road to deliverance. Disclosure of your addiction, combined with accountability, is an effective way to help you in your struggle to overcome sexual temptation and ultimately conquer your sexual addiction.

An accountability partner is someone who can love and care for you but at the same time, be brutally honest and tough on you when you need it. When I suggest an accountability partner or an accountability group to men, the first person most men think of is their best friend. This is only a good choice if he can meet the following criteria:

1. He must be anchored in a healthy and committed relationship with Christ.
2. He must truly desire to help and be accessible to you when you need him.

3. He must be able to commit time to pray for you and meet with you face to face on a regular basis.
4. He must be able to be discreet and confidential about the things that you share with him.
5. He must be someone you trust and respect.
6. He can't be afraid to address this issue head on.

If he is a true man of God, this will not be a problem. This friend needs to know God and have experienced His life-changing power in his own life in a personal way. It is essential that you partner with a man or men who know and understand this on a personal level. It bears repeating: you will not overcome this addiction without the power of God in your life.

An accountability partner is simply another brother in the Lord who is there to help you in your struggle through prayer, communication, guidance, and absolute honesty. He must be willing to be available to you at any time for any reason. The underlying reason that most men have no accountability partner is because being absolutely honest is not easy. To be transparent to another man or men, particularly in the area of your sexual sin, is difficult at best. Laying it all on the line is not a normal practice in most men's lives. This, believe it or not, is the beauty of accountability.

Accountability

Once you open up and pour out your struggles with your secret life, the healing can start. Secrets can keep you in bondage. Once you reveal those secrets, there is an indescribable peace that occurs. Simply stated, someone else is there to bear your burdens and to be an encouragement to you while they are holding your feet to the fire.

A weekly luncheon or meeting with your partner or partners is an excellent strategy. You need regular face-to-face involvement with a serious question and answer time as well as a time of sharing and encouraging one another. Remember your partners are there to help you, but at the same time, you are helping them as well. In my group, we don't deal with just sexual issues. We deal with the many aspects in our walk with Christ. It can include our personal finances and tithes, spiritual leadership or lack thereof within our families, as well as pornography and lust.

We always open in prayer and immediately follow that with a series of questions. Each week one of us is selected to ask these questions of each member of the group. You can develop your own line of questioning, but here are some of the questions that we use:

1. Since the last time we met, have you viewed any pornography on the Internet, in a magazine, on a video, DVD or television program?

2. Have you frequented any place of business where sex is marketed, i.e. a bookstore, topless bar, massage parlor or theatre?
3. Have you engaged in sex with anyone other than your wife?
4. Have you masturbated?
5. Have you been anywhere alone with someone from the opposite sex? where it could be perceived as inappropriate to others?
6. Have you been praying with your wife at night?
7. Have you been spending time reading the Word of God?
8. Are you paying your tithes?
9. Are you lying to me/us on any of these questions?

The immediate result of accountability is you will ALWAYS think first of your accountability partners and having to face them next week with negative answers. It makes it more difficult to get carried away with the lust process and act on it in a sinful way. It should be enough that we think of our heavenly Father and our families before we sin, but many times for whatever reason, that hasn't stopped us. This added element of three men who you have to look in the face and confess your sin to is a staggering reality and just one more safety net that may prevent you from acting out in a sinful way.

Accountability

The long-term result is that over time, as you get to learn more about each other and care and love one another, a real bond develops. It is like a bunch of war veterans getting together. There is no greater bond that occurs than when you have gone into battle together and looked out for the other man's backside. I liken this to a war because there is a real enemy out there whose sole purpose is to defeat you. Each man in your group knows this firsthand and wants nothing more than to succeed himself as well as to see you obtain success. You know that your group and the relationships within your group are working when you can call each other at any time or from anywhere for encouragement or prayer. Sometimes it is to talk someone out of acting on temptation at that exact moment.

One of my partners was out of town on a business trip and I received a call one evening. The voice said, "David, I am in a hotel room that has pornographic movies on pay per view. That little box has been calling out to me all night. I have just had a horrible day. I miss my family. I know I am going to fail tonight, so I just wanted to talk to you." He followed by apologizing for bothering me. I explained that no apology was required and he was doing exactly what we had talked about time and time again. We need to be there for each other in times of weakness. Sometimes we just need to pray over the phone line, or maybe we just need to talk to get our minds off of the temptation at hand. Whatever approach is taken, it is simply a cry for help to someone who can be trusted and can give some encouragement at that very moment.

My advice to my friend was to leave the hotel room and go down to the front desk and ask that the cable box be disconnected from his television. Then he was to call me back on his cell phone after that was accomplished. When he called back, I suggested he go out and have dinner at the Outback, come back to his room and go to sleep. He did as I suggested. But I didn't stop there. I tried to call the others in our group to have them pray, but unfortunately neither was home. So I immediately started to intercede on his behalf in prayer. I asked that God would protect his mind and thought process and give him the strength to overcome this seemingly insurmountable temptation that he was facing. To make a long story short, he didn't stumble that night or any other night during his trip.

This is the true essence of what an accountability partner is all about. It is being there for each other to strengthen one another when one of us is down. It is to pray with and remind each other of the real source of our power against temptation and lust. It is to be that rock when the foundation is slipping away.

One thing I have learned through this process is that temptation and lust comes and goes. Often it is short lived. If you can keep it in perspective and stifle it in a moment of temporary weakness, you will overcome it. The help of a partner at that moment when you think you can't resist can be all it takes to succeed.

I am a real believer in accountability groups. Not only will it help you to stay on the straight and narrow, but it will also help you to learn new ways to conquer through the experiences shared by others. You realize that we are all very much alike when it comes to lust. It is about taming the lust of the flesh and allowing the Spirit to control your life. Ultimately, these groups will develop men, who after having conquered their own issues, become so grateful for what God has in their life that they desire to help others. Some of the most effective ministries in dealing with sexual addicts are run by former addicts themselves. I can tell you that I receive no greater satisfaction in my walk than to know I have helped a fellow brother in the Lord to overcome his sexual addictions. You will feel the same way. My hope is that you too will act on it.

CHAPTER EIGHT

Level the Playing Field

"Therefore let him who thinks he stands take heed lest he fall. No temptation has overtaken you except such as is common to man; but God is faithful, who will not allow you to be tempted beyond what you are able, but with the temptation will also make the way of escape, that you may be able to bear it."
(1 Corinthians 10:12–13 NKJ)

It is no secret that we are bombarded with sex daily. In fact I think it is fair to say that we live in a sex-obsessed society. It is everywhere, on our television, radio, and in the workplace. It is regularly utilized in advertising products by both the electronic and printed media. It is becoming hard to watch a commercial and determine whether they are promoting the product or sex. Today, like no other time in our history, the female body is being exploited to generate interest in products and huge profits. Corporate America should be ashamed of the depths that they have allowed their advertising agencies to sink to in promoting their products and services.

This culture in which we live constantly throws sexuality in our face. It is hard to go through a day where you haven't been affected by its outreaching tentacles. This is why it is so important for men to level the playing field. You must take active steps to reduce the amount of temptation in your life. A recovering alcoholic doesn't keep beer in his refrigerator for obvious reasons. A recovering drug addict doesn't keep a hidden stash. You, likewise, should not keep anything in your home or office that may tempt you and potentially start the lust process. Remove anything that could be harmful to you. If you have an assortment of porn hidden somewhere in your house, you need to get rid of it now! If you are not willing to do this you are just kidding yourself and are not at all serious about deliverance from this problem. If it is your wife's mail order lingerie catalog, ask her to please throw it away. Whatever it is that may cause you to stumble or bring you difficulty, get rid of it!

In my opinion, no Christian man should allow premium cable channels into his home because late in the evening hours you can be assured that there will be nudity and content that you should not be viewing. Another good reason for not having these premium channels is so that your wife and children don't have the ability to view any of this filth as well. If you have basic cable and you know that there are programs on certain channels that negatively affect you, you need to program those channels out of your remote control. You need to be extremely careful of what videos and DVD's you rent. Their content can damage you and your family.

It is important to monitor the music you listen to. A diet of images, impulses, and music that is contrary to a Christ-led life will ultimately take you away from one. You need to avoid going near places that you have frequented in the past, such as topless bars or pornographic bookstores. You don't want to give Satan the opportunity to spark an image or memory that might start the lustful thought process to begin.

Anyone serious about protecting themselves from the Internet needs to invest in an Internet filtering system. This goes for both your home and work computer. These systems filter through the smut you are trying to avoid. I recommend the American Family Filter. It is a server-based system that is constantly updated and neither you nor any family member can override it. You can even have a report of the Internet sites you visited sent to your accountability partners. The annual cost is minimal and it is a small price to pay to protect you and your family from illicit material and chat rooms on the Internet. You can find it at *http://www.afafilter.com*.

If you have a computer in your home with Internet access, you should never put it in a private area. It should be out in the open for all to see and use. This is another small form of accountability. Never surf the net when your family is away or asleep. You are just asking for a large dose of temptation. I am a firm believer in having the same e-mail address as your wife. When someone communicates with my wife or myself via e-mail, they know it is available for both of us to read. We have no secrets in our house. Everything we receive is open and available for the other to read and view. This, I believe, is the ultimate form of accountability for both partners.

If you have received objectionable e-mails in the past and still continue to receive them, you need to change your e-mail address. Generally, you will receive these because of inappropriate chat rooms or web sites you have previously visited. By changing your address and sharing one address with your wife, you have eliminated temptation from unwanted e-mails. At the same time you have shown your wife that you are serious about purging your life of porn. This shows an incredible amount of sincerity and trust on your part to your wife. It will go a long way in mending any mistrust from previous failures.

I am a firm believer in the "garbage in, garbage out" theory of life. If you consume trash, you will in turn produce it mentally, verbally, and physically. This couldn't be more true than when dealing with sexuality. Each man must take the necessary steps to insulate himself from the attacks of the enemy. What you do with your free time, the forms of entertainment you choose, the places you choose to frequent, will all determine how serious you are about separating yourself from harmful influences. These influences will either ignite temptation or keep it away. Based on the failures of the past, you want to avoid temptation.

You must start a regime of daily prayer and reading the Word of God. You need to begin each day in prayer. Thank God for what He has and is continuing to do in your life. Secondly, ask His protection over you for the day ahead. Why is it we tend to pray only after we fall? We need to pray before the day begins and start the day in a state of worship and in touch with God, our source of strength. Only He can bring you through the day victorious. He wants you to trust in Him and Him alone. If you truly seek God with all your heart, mind, and spirit, He will provide a place of refuge and a source of power that will overcome any lust or temptation you may encounter. Begin your day with prayer and you will walk through your day with a song of victory in your heart.

When you are praying for your own protection for that day, also lift up your brothers in Christ who need the power of the Holy Spirit in their day as well. Something special happens when you concern yourself with another man's struggles. It takes your mind off your problems and can often make what you are dealing with seem pretty insignificant. There is enough power in the name of Jesus to go around for each of us. And just in case your brother forgot to pray to start his day, your sincere and earnest prayer for him may be just what he needs to get through his day.

Immerse yourself in the Word of God. As I have said before, it is powerful! When Jesus was in the wilderness and Satan came to tempt Him on three separate occasions, He responded each time by saying, "It is written." Of all the things that Jesus did during His ministry here on earth and with all the many experiences that could have been documented, why was this so important? It is so simple. The Son of the living God, with all His power, might, and majesty used scripture to rebuke and neuter Satan. It was a clear and flawless example of what we are to do when confronted with temptation.

"For the word of God is living and active. Sharper than any double-edged sword, it penetrates even to dividing soul and spirit, joints and marrow; it judges the thoughts and attitudes of the heart" (Hebrews 4:12 NIV). Scripture is but one more weapon we have to use against the enemy. Not only is it a weapon, but it acts as a purifier of your mind and senses. The Word of God, combined with the power of the Holy Spirit in your life, protects you. Use it to your best advantage and utilize it in times of temptation. Remember, you can't speak forth scripture if you don't take the time to read it. Memorize those scriptures that have made a difference in your life. You should be able to quote scripture during times of temptation because Satan will flee if you speak forth the Word of God. Make it a priority to read your Bible

daily and see if what I am telling you isn't true. You will not be disappointed.

You have heard it said, "An idle mind is the devil's playground." Gentlemen, you need to stay busy. When I was deep in my sexual addiction, I had a job that afforded me much freedom and extra time. As a commissioned salesman, you can work as hard or easy as you wish. I chose to work real hard at the beginning of the week and coast at the end. This made for free and easy Thursdays and wasted Fridays. With my problem this was the last thing I needed. Free time always got me into trouble. If you travel with your job, this can also make things difficult. For some reason, when we are away from familiar surroundings we tend to get even more free in our actions. We feel like no one will recognize us, so we try something new and different. Perhaps it is taking that next step in the addiction escalation or maybe getting bold enough to do something we never dreamed of doing on our own turf.

Whatever you do for a living and whether you travel or not, it is essential that you plan your time and not allow for large blocks of alone time. It is at these times when you can be at your weakest. It allows you time to entertain the lust process, fantasize, and eventually act on what you have been dwelling on. Plan your time after work around your wife and or family. Plan regular social functions with the men in your accountability group. It will refresh you and strengthen the group if you can meet and do things other than just in the accountability group setting.

You should quit socializing with anyone who has been a stumbling block to you in the past or lured you to do some of the very things you are trying to break free of. The environment and the people you choose to surround yourself with will either be a detriment or, in the case of Christian fellowship, strengthen you and lift you up. Surround yourself with people who love the Lord and have experienced His forgiveness and grace. It is that grace experienced firsthand that allows others to extend grace in return. God ministers to you through many sources other than just your pastor. Christian friends will often have just the right thing to say or the perfect scripture to share and lift your spirit. Never discount the value of godly friends. Make them a part of your daily life.

These are just a few of the many things that you can do. They are proactive steps to limit the opportunities of sexual temptation from entering your life on a daily basis. I have been speaking of the power of God continually throughout this book and how it is sufficient for you to be victorious. These common sense, preemptive strikes of holding temptation at bay will only serve to protect you further. The more you rid your life of the things that might draw you to act on lust, the sooner that sexual temptation will become a thing of the past. What you need to do is establish a whole new mind-set. This is achieved by taking your mind from the former preoccupation of sexual perversity to things of eternal value. "*Finally, brothers, whatever is true, what-*

ever is noble, whatever is right, whatever is pure, whatever is lovely, whatever is admirable—if anything is excellent or praiseworthy—think about such things" (Philippians 4:8 NIV).

Many of these suggestions entail involvement with other people, specifically believers. I know that this is something most of you will drag your feet in doing, but it is essential that you bite the bullet and force yourself to do it. The reason that this is so difficult to do is simple. You have just come out of THE MOST SELFISH of all addictions. Addiction to porn and sex is the purest form of self-gratification that there is. This is why you have remained so quiet and not shared it with a soul up until now. You insulated yourself from the world and people who care because you have been consumed with sex. It is vitally important to change this trend in your life. Openness and accountability is what will keep you on the road to complete recovery. Surrounding yourself with good people with the right influence, combined with honesty in your struggle and service to others, will result in success.

Throughout the Bible, when Jesus healed people or delivered them from an insurmountable situation, He never seemed to repeat or duplicate the method that He used. Whenever He performed a miracle, whether it was giving sight to the blind, making the lame to walk, casting out demons or bringing the dead back to life, it was always a bit different. I believe that it was done that way by design. It was to show us that we are all different in our levels of faith and that there are as many difficulties to face in this life as there are people. It also proves that God is never predictable. I mention this because I believe that most of us living in America have what I refer to as a "fast-food mentality." We want a quick fix to everything, including our innermost shortcomings and battles. We look to others and their positive experiences to measure and guide our approach to deliverance. But the simple truth is that God will deal with each of us in a way that is meaningful and ultimately successful for us.

I have tried to lay out for you a process that, in my life, brought about complete and total deliverance from my sexual addiction and perversity. This is not to suggest that God will deal with you in exactly the same method or ways. Chances are, He will do a different work in your life. God knows what makes you tick. He knows the number of hairs on your head. He knew you while you were being formed in the womb. He knows exactly what you need to overcome. This is why it is essential that you spend most of your time seeking God. He will guide your steps and show you the areas in your life that need to be changed. The most important thing is that you listen and act upon it accordingly.

"Trust in the Lord with all your heart, and lean not on your own understanding; in all your ways acknowledge Him and He shall direct your paths" (Proverbs 3:5–6 NKJ). If you put your complete trust and faith in God and follow the path set out for you, you will obtain victory over this consuming addiction. Your

obedience to God will ultimately determine your outcome. You really need to put it all on the line and see that God is faithful and true. He wants you to pursue Him with as much fervor and desire as you used to pursue the things of this world. Simply put, He wants your all. When you bring yourself to this point of giving Him your all, you will not believe the life that He in turn will give you.

CHAPTER NINE

Walk in the Spirit Deny the Flesh

"I say then; Walk in the Spirit, and you shall not fulfill the lust of the flesh. For the flesh lusts against the Spirit, and the Spirit against the flesh; and these are contrary to one another, so that you do not do the things that you wish."

(Galatians 6:16–17 NKJ)

Flesh versus Spirit. It is the authentic, real-life scenario of good versus evil. It is Christ versus Satan. The two are diametrically opposed as the Word states, "contrary to one another." You have probably heard at some time in your life about walking in the Spirit and not in the flesh. I never really understood what it meant. I had this image of a guy walking around in some kind of semi-conscious state, chanting prayers, and being so spiritually superior that he was of no earthly good. This was something that I wanted nothing to do with.

When I recommitted my life to Christ, I had a new-found desire to know more about the power of the Holy Spirit. My hunger for God and His righteousness led me to understand what walking in the Spirit meant and how it changed my life. I want to share what it means to me and how it has affected my walk and ability to deny my flesh.

The man walking in the flesh lives by feeding and nurturing his flesh. He is quite simply self-absorbed. His flesh needs to be entertained and requires stimulation and attention. The flesh wants to be satisfied first and foremost and takes a back seat to no one. It never wants to be denied and it knows no discipline. The flesh never considers any consequence that may arise from its feeding frenzy. It lives only for today to quench insatiable desires.

There comes a point in a man's life when he has fed the flesh to such a degree that the flesh now controls him. The flesh is in the driver's seat, taking direction from no one, including your conscience and even the conviction of the Holy Spirit. The flesh tunes out and overrides any dissenting voice of reason with regard to lust or sexual sin. This is walking in the flesh and not in the Spirit.

Please understand this. There is no Spirit man or walking in the Spirit until you have asked Christ to be the Lord of your life. When you accept Him as your Savior, His precious Holy Spirit resides in you. The by-product of the Holy Spirit in your life is the fruit of the Spirit. "*But the fruit of the Spirit is love, joy, peace, patience, kindness, goodness, faithfulness, gentleness and self-control*" (Galatians 5:22 NIV). When it comes to sexual sin, self-control is probably the most coveted. This fruit doesn't just happen. It grows like anything else. You don't simply wake up one day and possess all of these qualities. The Holy Spirit has planted these seeds in you but you must feed, nurture, and cultivate the Spirit man to see them grow. This fruit is the manifestation of the believer's character. It is the divine nature of Christ working within us.

As in every other aspect of our life, God has given us the ability to make our own decisions. It is called free will. He allows us to either accept or reject Him. The Holy Spirit draws us to Christ but ultimately, we decide whether we will serve Him or not. Likewise, this same free will exists when it comes to the level of commitment in our walk with Christ. Do you just want to get by knowing that you have salvation or do you strive to grow deeper in your walk? The depth of your relationship with Christ will determine your ability to walk in the Spirit and deny the flesh.

The power of the Holy Spirit in your life and the fruit thereof, can only be limited by you. The Holy Spirit will not prevent you from getting angry, but He will remind you that it is wrong before you lash out at someone. The Holy Spirit will not stop you from acting out sexual sin but, He will convict you before you make the choice to do so. The man who walks in the Spirit is one who hears the warnings from the Holy Spirit, grasps hold of His power and responds accordingly. He does not grieve the Holy Spirit by tuning Him out. The Spirit man knows the voice of God, honors and reacts positively to it. He flees from sin and shuts down the lust process before the flesh man can entertain it.

I regularly talk with Christian men who say that they cannot control their sexual desires. They fall time and time again and continually live in defeat. After further discussions, I ask what they are doing to strengthen their walk in Christ. The predictable answer is: "Aside from attending a church service once a week, absolutely nothing." Gentlemen, if your level of commitment to Christ is based solely on going to church once a week, it is no wonder you live a defeated life. I don't say this out of disrespect to your pastor, I say this out of first-hand knowledge. It is impossible, let me say it again, *impossible*, to have the power it takes to overcome the flesh daily without seeking and dwelling in His presence daily.

> *"Now to him who is able to do immeasurably more than all we ask or imagine, according to His power that is at work within us."*
> (Ephesians 3:20 NIV)

The words, "According to His power that is at work within us" tells a story. I understand it to mean that His power working in my life may be less or more than the power at work within someone else's.

What I am trying to convey to you is this: the degree in which the fruit of the Spirit is present and active in your life will be determined by your openness to the Holy Spirit. The power of the Spirit within you is limitless. It can make your current struggles disappear. It is all you need to live a victorious life.

To walk in the Spirit you must be Spirit minded. The secret to effective fruit bearing and walking in the Spirit is abiding in Christ. Jesus said, *"I am the vine, you are the branches. He who abides in me, and I in him, bears much fruit; for without Me you can do nothing. If anyone does not abide in Me, he is cast out as a branch and is withered; and they gather them and throw them into the fire, and they are burned. If you abide in Me, and My words abide in you, you will ask what you desire, and it shall be done for you"* (John 15: 5–7 NKJ). You must spend each day in communion with God. This is done in three ways: prayer, praise, and reading the Word.

I start every day with prayer and praise. I believe in wishing my heavenly Father a good morning and praising Him for who He is and all He has done in my life. I thank Him for His many blessings and ask for His continued protection for that day. I ask Him for protection for my mind, my thought processes and against the wiles of the evil one. I often follow the scripture found in Ephesians chapter six where the apostle Paul spoke of putting on the armor of God. I ask Him to gird my waist with truth, protect me with the breastplate of righteousness, shod my feet with the gospel of peace, and quench the fiery arrows of Satan with the shield of faith. I ask Him to apply the helmet of salvation and the sword of the Spirit to my life for the upcoming day. I even visualize myself applying that armor to my body as protection.

I listen exclusively to Christian music on my way to and from work. I do not want anything to side-track my mind away from Christ. I enjoy listening to praise and worship music as it builds a foundation of praise that sets the tone for the day ahead. I use that hour commute every morning to commune with God. This puts my day into His hands and it keeps me focused on spiritual things. It puts me in a mind-set where temptation is not present. But if temptation should come, it equips me with the power to overcome.

You must make time to spend with God. Any relationship requires communication and nurturing. I am sure that all of you have had a relationship in your life that you allowed to dissolve due to lack of effort. This often occurs when you relocate and now this friend does not cross your path anymore. The old saying goes, "Out of sight is out of mind." Over time, it just dwindles due to a lack of communication and, from time away from each other. The same thing holds true in your relationship with Christ. If you don't take the time to talk with Jesus in prayer or read His Word, He can become that lost friend. This does not occur because of Christ, it occurs because of you. You are the one who has moved and forgotten the most treasured Friend of your life.

As mentioned earlier, reading the Word of God is a requirement for success in your Christian walk. I cannot stress it enough! It is essential to your well-being. The Word of God is described throughout the Bible in terms that prove its importance. *"Your Word I have hidden in my heart, that I might not sin against You"* (Psalm 119:11 NKJ). *"Your Word is a lamp to my feet and a light to my path"* (Psalm 119:105 NKJ). It is described as *"fire"* and *"like a hammer that breaks the rock in pieces"* (Jeremiah 23:29 NKJ), and as *"living and powerful, and sharper than any two-edged sword"* (Hebrews 4:12 NKJ). It is called the *"Sword of the Spirit"* (Ephesians 6:17 NKJ).

There are many more references to the power of scripture in the Word of God. It is very important in the life of a believer. This should be a clear indication that you need to partake in a regular study of the Word, as it is essential to victorious living. Filling your spirit with the written Word of God will bring to your remembrance words of life in times of struggle and temptation. Once you have memorized scripture, you can quote it during these times and they will enable you to overcome.

Any professional worth his weight will continue to read and educate himself about advancements in his line of work throughout his career. To be effective, he will read trade journals and articles to keep him on the cutting edge and a step in front of his competition. A world-class athlete will daily push his body to its physical limits in order to raise the threshold of those limits. He exercises his muscles so that atrophy will not set in and render him ineffective. This is the same approach that you need to take as a believer in Christ. You must continue to feed your spirit with things of the Spirit and sharpen your skills as though your very life depended on it because it does. It may not be not physical life and death, but it certainly is spiritual life or death.

The Word of God is the ultimate trade publication in the walk of life. It is a love letter from our heavenly Father to answer the many mysteries of life. It is designed to keep us on the cutting edge of a righteous life and to assure success in our walk with Him.

Your struggles with porn and sexual addiction can be overcome when you decide to walk in the Spirit and be Spirit minded and not carnal minded. You have a choice to make and once again, it boils down to desire. You must desire Christ and His righteousness far above your past desires for sexual gratification. It is more simple than you think. When you seek God with all of your being, He naturally becomes the focus of your life. You will desire to please Him above pleasing the carnal minded man inside. When Christ is the focus of your day, you will find that past temptations rarely surface. And if they do, you have the ability to overcome through the power of the Holy Spirit which is vibrant and active in your life.

Walking in the Spirit and not in the flesh is a spiritual state that can be attained in the life of any man. It is not attained by your own strength, but through the power of the Holy Spirit active within the life of an obedient and willing vessel committed to following Christ. It should be the desire of your heart and something you strive to attain. Once you have experienced it, you will no longer be controlled by the flesh. Keeping your flesh in check becomes a daily certainty. The Spirit man will be calling the shots and will ultimately prevail because it is *"Not by might nor by power, but by my Spirit, says the Lord of hosts"* (Zechariah 4:6 NKJ).

CHAPTER TEN

Keep on Pouring

"When all the jars were full, she said to her son, 'Bring me another one.' But he replied, 'There is not a jar left.' Then the oil stopped flowing."

(2 Kings 4:6 NIV)

Whatever process of change God brings you through in your deliverance from sexual addiction, you need to give back to others some of the blessings that God is pouring into your life. Get involved in the work of the Lord. Start at your very own church. First of all, I'm not aware of a church that couldn't use the help. Secondly, when you involve yourself in helping others, it takes your attention off of your own struggles and puts the focus on the needs of others. Thirdly, involving yourself in the ministry will help you to develop friendships with other Christian men in your church.

These are the kind of relationships you need right now.

At my church we have a program called Adopt a Block. This is where we go out into the neighborhood and clean up yards, haul away trash, and see if we can meet the many needs that these families have. It is simply taking on the heart of a servant and earning their trust and confidence. This makes for a much better listener when sharing your faith. We bring much-needed food to families who need some help. Ultimately, we share the gospel message with them and make arrangements to bus them in to our church on Sundays.

I will never forget my first time out. We took some toys that, by most people's standards, would be considered well worn. As we went into the homes of these poor people who could barely get by, we handed out the toys to their children. You would have thought we were giving away a million dollars. The joy that filled these children's eyes was priceless. At the same time, it filled me with mixed emotions. I was glad that I was there bringing a smile to the face of a precious child, but I was also sad that any child would have to live in such horrible conditions and poverty.

I remember calling my wife as I was driving home. She knew immediately that I was crying and asked me what was wrong. I explained to her what I had experienced that day and she cried with me. I vividly remember telling her that if she ever heard me complain about things we couldn't afford, or if I ever started feeling sorry for myself, to reach out and smack me back into reality. I learned a lot about myself that day and how self-absorbed I can be. I also learned that there is nothing more special than being used of God and helping others. I call it pouring into others.

In 2 Kings chapter four, the prophet Elijah was approached by a widow who was severely in debt. She was about to lose her home, but even worse, potentially her two sons. In those days it was difficult, if not impossible, for a woman to support herself, let alone two boys plus keep a roof over their heads. It was also legal for a debtor to actually take her sons from her to work off the debt that her deceased husband had accumulated. She was in need of a miracle. She knew that Elijah had been involved in many miraculous situations before, so she sought out the prophet of God.

Elijah asked her what she had in the house. She simply replied that she had only a small jar of oil. Oil had value, but this small quantity was barely enough to use in preparing a meal or lighting a lamp. Elijah, however, needed a starting point and that little jar of oil was just what he needed to bring about a stretching of her faith. It was merely a tool that God used to provide the much-needed miracle in her life.

When God asks us what we have to offer, the answer is often, "Nothing." For some reason, we believe that we have nothing of value—no qualities or gifts that God can use to help others with. But all

He is looking for is a willing vessel. When you allow yourself to be a willing servant and be an extension of God's love to others, the blessings that follow are too great to contain. Do not allow yourself to be deceived. You have much to offer God. Allowing the use of your time and talents for His cause is a starting point for your own healing. When you are being used of God, the greatest blessings go directly to you. Most Christians don't see it that way because they have never put themselves in a position to see it come to pass. I want you to put yourself in that position!

Elijah asked the widow and her sons to go and collect some containers from their neighbors and bring as many as they could find. The Bible never says just how many containers they brought, but I can assure you that if they had brought a thousand, each one would have been filled. Elijah told her to pour her small jar of oil into one of the large containers that she had borrowed. As she started to pour, the oil just kept pouring out until the large vessel was full. Then she went to the next vessel and filled that one. This went on and on until every container that was presented was completely full! The Bible says that the widow had enough oil to pay all of her debts, which kept her sons from being taken from her. She even had some left over! This was truly a miracle from God and just what this widow needed.

I look at this story and I view the participants to be like you and me. We may not be losing our home or our children, but we too have a huge need that only God can provide. If the widow had not been obedient to the prophet of God, she would never have received her miracle. Likewise, if we are obedient to God, our miracle will also come. I believe the deliverance we are seeking from sexual addiction lies within our ability and desire to serve God with everything we have and to be an instrument used by Him. Like the widow, as we pour what little we have, God gives us more. He multiplies our resources and soon we are doing more than we ever thought possible for His kingdom.

It is during this time of giving that God supernaturally wipes away the desires and temptations that we been consumed with in the past. Soon you will find that it is not about you anymore. And that, my friend, has been the problem all along. This whole addiction and consumption of porn and other sexually related smut has been self-serving, self-gratifying, and self-indulgent. Simply put, you have been consumed in your own flesh, feeding, nurturing, and perpetuating a selfish life. Getting involved in a cause for Christ will unlock the yoke that has bound you for too long.

Like the widow, as we pour out of ourselves into others, God pours into us. She was only limited by the amount of vessels that her faith allowed her to gather. Once there were no more vessels to pour into, the oil stopped, but not before her needs were first met. We will never run out of vessels to pour into. The world is just too large and the needs are too vast. There is a hurting world out there that needs

God and the forgiveness and hope that only He brings. Will you allow yourself to quit thinking about you and start thinking about others? When you do, the problems you are currently facing will seem so small. What a tremendous testimony it is when God does great things in and through the life of an obedient man who is sold out to Him.

God is using me to reach out to men who are dealing with sexual addiction. As I pour what little I have to offer, God is blessing me tremendously. I want to challenge you to step out in faith and act upon what God is calling you to do. Ask God to forgive you of the perverted lifestyle that you have been living. Take the needed steps to reduce the amount of temptation you allow into your life. Commit yourself to start praying and reading the Word of God daily. Seek and learn how to walk in the Spirit and not in the flesh. Then, a very common side effect will occur. You will desire desperately to be used by God in whatever way He needs you. This will be the crowning and final step to your complete and total deliverance from sex and porn addiction. You will replace your desire for the things of this world with a greater desire for the things of God. This is where you need to be.

I hope you have found the information in this book to be helpful. My prayer is that it has challenged and motivated you to change the way you live your life. Maybe you are thinking that it is good that God helped David from his struggle but He could never bring me out of where I am. If you are thinking this, you are sorely mistaken. Satan will do everything in his power to keep you defeated and thinking that there is no help for you. Nothing could be further from the truth.

There are so many things that I have not shared with you, particularly where my addiction had taken me. I can't share it all with you because there is just too much to tell. Details and experiences aren't always beneficial. In fact, they can be problematic to some who are struggling with this problem. But I can tell you that when I am ministering to men who are dealing with a sexual addiction the first words out of my mouth are, "There is nothing you can share with me today that will shock me. I have heard it all and chances are I have already been there and done that." I do this to relax and make them feel that they can be open and honest with me. Another reason for saying this is because I want them and you to know that my problems were severe. At the same time I want to build hope and a determined understanding that God can change their life as He did mine.

This addiction was the driving force in my life and it cost me dearly. It resulted in a failed marriage and a loss of many friendships. It destroyed my self-worth, my integrity, and deteriorated the trust that some held in me. I was burdened financially with staggering debt; my pursuit of sexual gratification consumed most all of my free time. Most importantly, it nearly cost me my soul.

But my God is a God of second chances. He has given me a life that I never thought was within my reach. He forgave me of my sins and put my feet on a path that has been never ending and ever growing. To be free of the chains that were binding me through sexual addiction is an unexplainable relief. There is a complete feeling of freedom unlike anything I have ever known.

God had a plan for my life. It took my surrendering it all to Him before He could truly start this work that is still in progress. He has blessed me with the most incredible wife that a man could ask for. I shared everything from my past with her. In spite of it all, her trust in me is unwavering. These past seven years with her have been the best years of my life. God has blessed us with a beautiful child and we all live in a home where we honor God and continually praise Him for everything He has done in our lives.

I am on staff at one of the largest soul-winning churches in America and in my opinion, working with the greatest pastor in the world. He is a lover of people and is such an inspiration and encouragement to me. I never dreamed that the darkness of my past would be turned around and developed into a ministry that reaches out to hurting men who, like myself, needed a new lease on life.

God has a plan for you as well. But I have one question for you. Are you ready to put it all on the line? Look at my life and know that the same God who healed and delivered me from the trap that I was in wants to do the same for you! It is now time for you to act. Please do not put it off any longer. You must first invite Him into your heart and make Him the number one priority of your life. This is where God belongs. This is the only place He can be in order to do a new work in your life. Don't wait another day. Victory is at hand. Reach out and grasp it with all of your might and let God show you the greatness of His redeeming power!

Notes

1. American Broadcasting Company, Prime Time with Diane Sawyer. Program aired, January 23, 2003.

2. Maryland Coalition Against Pornography, Silver Springs, Maryland, Website *www.mcap1.com*. Accessed May 29, 2002.

3. Janet Chismar, *Pornography Addiction: A Stronghold Inside Church Walls Too*. *www.crosswalk.com*. On-line article, accessed March 5, 2002.

4. Tim Wilkins of Cross Ministries, "No Wonder They Call it . . . The Web" *www.afa.net.* Online article, accessed March 5, 2002.

5. Maryland Coalition Against Pornography, Silver Springs, Maryland, *www.mcap1.com,* 1997.

6. Janet Chismar, *Pornography Addiction: A Stronghold Inside Church Walls Too. www.crosswalk.com.* On-line article, accessed March 5, 2002.

7. Patrick Means. Results of a confidential survey conducted by and reported in *Men's Secret Wars,* Fleming H. Revell, a division of Baker Book House Company, Grand Rapids, MI, 1996, 1999.

8. Dr. Victor Cline. This was a conclusion from scientific research as cited in a speech titled: *Cyber Secrets The Problem of Pornography: Pornography Effects and Ultimate Consequences,* presented at Brigham Young University, February, 2001..

9. Thomas Parker, Director of Psychology, The Family Workshop, Austin Texas; 1989 South-

ern Baptist Christian Life Commission. Excerpt
from the CLC annual seminar proceedings.

10. Dolph Zillman and Jennings Bryant. This is
a conclusion from clinical research reported
in *Pornography: Research Advances and Policy
Considerations,* published by Lawrence
Erlbaum Associates, Hillsdale, NJ, 1989.

To order additional copies of

THE SECRET
IN THE PEW

Have your credit card ready and call:

1-877-421-READ (7323)

or please visit our web site at
www.pleasantword.com

Also available at: www.amazon.com

CPSIA information can be obtained at www.ICGtesting.com
Printed in the USA
BVOW021700190412

288111BV00001B/10/A